zendoodle pocket coloring

Enchanting Gardens

Other great books in the series

zendoodle coloring

zendoodle pocket coloring

Calming Swirls

Creative Sensations

zendoodle coloring

Calming Swirls

Creative Sensations

Enchanting Gardens

Inspiring Zendalas

Keep Calm and Color On

Keep Happy and Color On

Keep Merry and Color On

zendoodle pocket coloring

Enchanting Gardens

Captivating Florals to Color and Display

illustrations by

Nikolett Corley

ST. MARTIN'S GRIFFIN
NEW YORK

ZENDOODLE POCKET COLORING: ENCHANTING GARDENS.

Printed in the United States of America. For information, address St. Martin's Press, 175 Fifth Avenue, New York, N.Y. 10010.

www.stmartins.com

ISBN 978-1-250-10513-4 (trade paperback)

St. Martin's Griffin books may be purchased for educational, business, or promotional use. For information on bulk purchases, please contact the Macmillan Corporate and Premium Sales Department at 1-800-221-7945, extension 5442, or write to specialmarkets@macmillan.com.

First Edition: January 2016

10 9 8 7 6 5 4 3 2 1

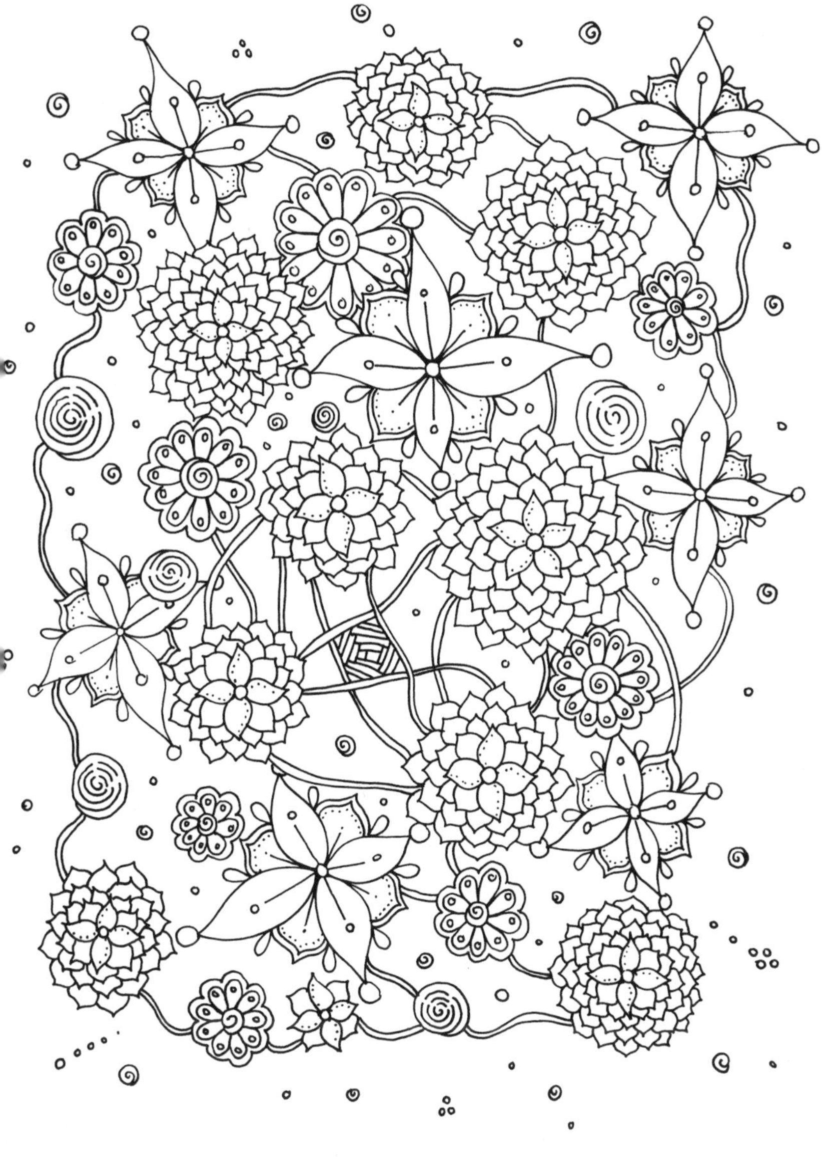

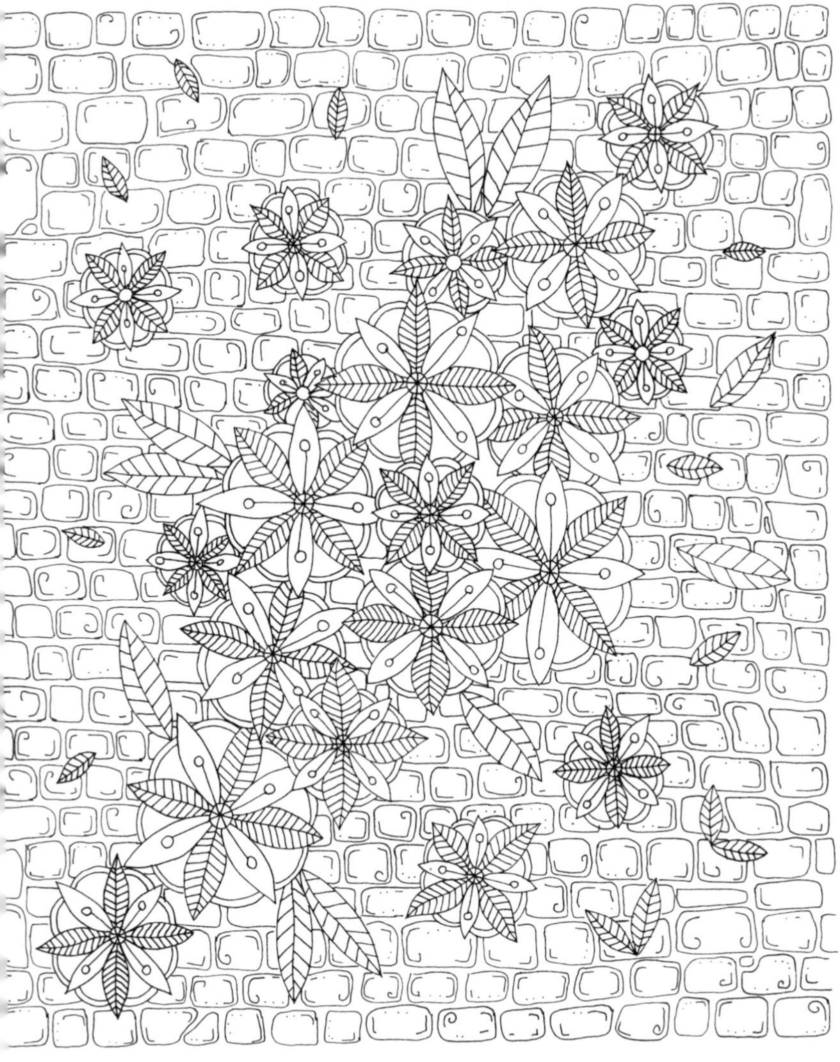